HISTORY OF

# THE BLACK MAN

## Joseph Julius Jackson

An Authentic Collection of Historical Information on the Early Civilization of
the Descendants of Ham,
the Son of Noah.

History of the Black Kingdoms of Ghana,
Melle, Songhay and Hansas, and
the Early American Negro.

ISBN: 978-1-63923-235-2

Printed: June 2022

Cover Art By: Amit Paul

Published and Distributed By:Lushena Books
607 Country Club Drive, Unit E
Bensenville, IL 60106
www.lushenabooksinc.com/books

ISBN: 978-1-63923-235-2

# HISTORY OF
# THE BLACK MAN

## Joseph Julius Jackson

An Authentic Collection of Historical Information on the Early Civilization of
the Descendants of Ham,
the Son of Noah.

---

History of the Black Kingdoms of Ghana,
Melle, Songhay and Hansas, and
the Early American Negro.

---

## THIRD EDITION

---

COMPILED BY
### REV. J. J. JACKSON, D. D.
BELLEFONTAINE, OHIO.

---

# INTRODUCTORY

It is very essential that every race should possess a correct knowledge of its own past history.

The masses of the American negro have been deprived of the opportunity of obtaining an adequate knowledge of the past history of the black man. The average historian has not considered the ancient history of the black man of sufficient importance to claim his attention. Even Mr. Myers would have the students of his general history believe that the black man has always been a hewer of wood and a drawer of water. A large majority of the men of letters of our own people who are very proficient in ancient, medieval and modern history of Greece, Rome, and even China, Japan, and other European and Asiatic countries, know very little of the history of their own people.

A lack of historical knowledge of ourselves has been the means of lessening of our race pride. A better knowledge of the contribution of the black man to civilization will cause us to have a better opinion of ourselves. At considerable expense and with much labor and research, the writer has succeeded in collecting what he considers a great deal of valuable information, which he has placed in this little book and given to the public at a cost within the reach of everyone who desires valuable information upon the past and present history of the black man. A brief reference will be made to the origin of the race, the rise of the Ethiopian and Egypt, and the early influence of African civilization upon the ancient history of the world. Considerable space will be given to the black kingdoms of Soudan and the high degree of civilization which was found to exist among them before the arrival of white explorers. The following are some of the kingdoms to which reference will be made at some length: namely: Ghana, Melle, Songhay and Hansas. It will also be shown that Spain was ruled by a black dynasty of Africa for more than half a century, 1086-1147. Much space will be given to the history of the American negro, 1619 to the present date. Books containing much of the information found in this book are not accessible to the masses of the people. I am aware that much of the information found in this book will sound like a fairy tale, but I assure the readers that every word is authenic history.

In dealing with the black kingdoms and people of Soudan, I have selected the black type of the race, to the exclusion of the mixed races, to refute the argument that civilization is the heritage of the lighter race. It will also be shown that the native Africans whose history we relate in this book are not naked savages of whom we have heard so much, but they are people who have always worn clothes and lived in stately mansions. Mrs. Shaw, ("Lady Lugard") in the introduction to her book, entitled "A Tropical Dependency," has the following to say: "The traveler on the Niger River, from its source to Sokoto, leaves the naked savage of the coast to prowl in his dusky nakedness through the mangrove swamps of

Southern Nigeria; at its mouths. He sees natives on its banks, ever increasing in dignity as the latitude recedes from the equator. At Lokoja no native is unclothed. A little farther north, at Bida, where the town is approached by avenues of trees, native brass and glass manufacturers add to the usual industries. Moorish dress is already the fashion. In the markets of Sokoto and Kano the scenery is as varied and as dignified as any market in the Mediterranean coast.

REV. J. J. JACKSON, D. D.

Bellefontaine, Ohio

March 23, 1921.

# History of the Black Man

It is generally conceded that all the families of the human race had a common parentage in Noah. Noah had three sons, Shem, Ham and Japheth. It was the original purpose of God that these three men should be the heads of separate and distinct nations. The carrying out of this purpose was begun by the confusion of language at the tower of Babel. Each of these men and their descendants were given a distinct language so that they no longer spoke their mother tongue. Ham had four sons, viz: Cush, Mizraim, Phut and Caanan. Babalonia, Phonecia, Arabia, Caanan, Syria and Africa were settled by the descendants of Ham. Nimrod, the mighty hunter and founder of cities, was the son of Cush and the grandson of Ham.

Historians tell us that the inscriptions upon the tablets and submerged towers and monuments of Babylon, Egypt and Ethiopia, reveal the fact that they all spoke the same language. Phut, Mizraim and Cush settled Africa. Scholars agree that Arabia was first peopled by Cush and his descendants, Baamah or Raamah and Sabtah. After settling Arabia, Cush migrated cross the Red Sea, if indeed the Red Sea existed at that early period, and settled Ethiopia, which lies south of Egypt. Students of history concede that the Arabs and the races of Africa are near kinsmen. Ethiopia and Egypt are regarded as the oldest settlements upon the African continent. Historically they are the eldest born of all time; the

mothers of all subsequent civilization; the longest lived
among nations of the earth; the teachers of art, philos-
ophy and religion, before Greece and Rome were born.
When everywhere else rude huts and primitive tents
were mankind's highest form of architecture, Ethiopia
and Egypt were rearing their stupendous pyramids and
temples, which still remain the marvel of the world.

The Ethiopian represents the black type of the
Hametic race. "Can the leper change his spots or the
Ethiopian his skin?" is a familiar Bible quotation. All
of the Hametic races have either black or dark skins, or
have either wooly or curly hair. The Egyptians vary in
color from black to yellow brown. The civilization of
Ethiopia is perhaps older than that of Egypt. Heeren
historical researches: African races, has the following to
say: "In Nubia and Ethiopia, stupendous, numerous and
primeval monuments proclaim so loudly a civilization
contemporary to, aye, earlier than that of Egypt, that it
may be accepted with the greatest confidence that the
arts, sciences and religion descended from Nubbia to the
lower country of Mizraim; that civilization descended to
the Nile, built Memphis, and finally, sometime later,
wrested by colonization, the delta from the sea."

The fame of the Ethiopian was widespread in ancient history. Herodotus describes them as the tallest,
the most beautiful and the longest lived of the human
race, and before Herodotus Homer describes them as the
most just of men and the favorites of the gods. All the
purely African, or black families, are either descendants
of Ethiopia or Egypt.

Having briefly considered the origin of the black

family, I shall next give a short history of some of the
black kingdoms of Africa.

---

## CHAPTER II

Ethiopia and Egypt are the oldest and most re-
nowned of all the black kingdoms.

The history of these ancient kingdoms is so well
known that it will not be necessary to give them any more
than a passing notice.   In art, science, literature, government and law these ancient kingdoms have reached a degree of perfection which subsequent ages have not been
able to surpass.   The obelisk, sphinxes and pyramids are
stupendous works of human achievements, unrivaled by
any of the work of modern times.   The ruins of Thebes,
the most ancient of Egyptian cities, reveal the high degree
of civilization to which these kingdoms had attained.

In speaking of this ancient city, the late Dr. J. H.
Barrows, who was president of Oberlin University, has
the following to say: The plain was not only adorned by
large and handsome dwellings, for man, but by temples
and palaces of whose grandeur words can give but a faint
conception.

All of the civilized nations of the world are vieing
with each other in collecting relics of that ancient yet
most advanced civilization of more than 6000 years ago.

With much labor and at great expense, New York
City has succeeded in bringing across the continents the
great obelisk erected by Thothsmes III.   It now stands in
Central Park, New York, near 17th Street and 5th Ave-
nue.

For at the base of this same shaft of stone the Pharaohs of 5000 years ago and of subsequent periods were wont to stand and read the inscriptions that told of their greatness as well as the greatness of the entire Egyptian kingdom.

We shall now pass from the known kingdoms of ancient Ethiopia and Egypt to the hitherto unknown kingdoms of Soudan.

During the 8th century of our present Christian era there flourished a very important town in western Soudan by the name of Ghana. Its exact location is not definitely known. It was perhaps a few days' journey from Timbuctoo.

After being wrested from the hands of the Burburs in the earlier part of the 8th century A. D., it was ruled over by a long list of powerful black kings.

In speaking of Ghana, Mrs. Shaw ("Lady Lugard") says: The town had several mosques and other public buildings and the houses generally were very elegant.

The people were rich and living in great comfort.

The king's residence was a well built castle, thoroughly fortified, decorated inside by sculptures and pictures, and having glass windows. When the king gave audience to the people he appeared in great state, seated under a pavilion, round which ranged ten horses caparisoned in gold. Behind him were ten pages bearing shields and swords mounted in gold.

Gold was so plentiful and salt so scarce that the former was exchanged for its weight of the latter. The king possessed a nugget of gold which weighed thirty pounds.

El-Idrisi writing of this kingdom, says: Ghana is the most considerable, the most thickly populated, and the

most commercial of all the black countries. It is visited
by rich merchants of all the surrounding countries and
from the extremities of the west.

The king had a standing army of 200,000 men. He
is described as being one of the most just of men, whose
custom it was to ride once daily into the poorest and most
wretched parts of the city, and there dispense justice to
all who had reason for complaint.

On all other occasions he rode in great pomp, mag-
nificently dressed in silk and jewels, surrounded by
guards, preceded by elephants, giraffes and other wild
animals of Soudan, and no one dared to approach him.
The influence of this powerful kingdom extended to
Egypt, North Africa, and even to Spain in Europe.

### The Millestinean Kingdom

Millestean was another influential black kingdom
of the Soudan.   This kingdom reached the zenith of its
power after its kings had accepted the Mohammedan religion, which took place during the 11th century.   The
Millestinean Empire reached the heighth of its influence
under the rulership of Mansamusa.   Mansa means king.
After this powerful black king had established peace and
prosperity throughout the length and breadth of his vast
domain, he made his celebrated pilgrimage to Mecca in
the year 1324.   The caravan consisted on this occasion,
we are told, of no less than 60,000 persons.   The baggage
of this caravan was generally carried by camels, but
12,000 slaves formed the personal retinue of Mansamusa.
All these were dressed in tunics of brocade or Persian
silk.   When he rode, 500 of them marched before him,
carrying a staff of pure gold which weighed sixty-two

ounces. The remainder carried the royal baggage. The caravan was supplied with all essential luxuries, including good cooks, who prepared elaborate dishes, not only for the king, but for the king's friends at every halting place. To defray the expenses of this journey the king took with him gold dust to the value of upwards of a million sterling or five million dollars. This was carried in eighty camel loads, of three hundred pounds each. In making this pilgrimage he made it convenient to pass through his entire kingdom, stopping on every Friday to build a mosque for the people. He went by the way of Egypt where he spent considerable time with the Sultan and learned men of that country. He finally reached Meca, where he made many literary acquaintances, and persuaded Abu-Ishak, the Spanish poet and architect, to return with him. While at Meca it is said that he erected a very beautiful mosque. He returned by a different route, thus enabling him to pass through all parts of his empire. Having made a complete round of his empire, he re-entered his capital and immediately employed his Spanish architect to design for him a hall of audience, built after the fashion of Egyptian architecture.

It is stated that Abu-Ishak displayed all the wonders of his genius in the erection of an admirable monument which gave great satisfaction to the king. The hall was square and surrounded by a dome. It was built of stone, covered with plaster and decorated with beautiful, colored arabesques. It had also two tiers of arched windows, of which the lower windows were framed in gold plated upon wood, while the upper ones were framed in silver plated upon wood. This hall of audience communicated with the palace by an interior door. After

returning from his pilgrimage to Meca, Mansamusa
turned his arms against Timbuctoo, and finally took pos-
session of the town in 1336.    Musa made Timbuctoo the
capital of his empire.    He made the town magnificent
with a royal palace and mosque, which he built.    These
buildings were designed by the architect Abu-Ishak, and
were built of cut stone.    The remains of this palace exist until the present day.

We will give fuller description of Timbuctoo fur-
ther on.

Mansamusa had a very prosperous reign of twenty-
five years.    Ibu Khaldien says of him: Mansamusa was
distinguished by his ability and by the holiness of his life.
The justice of his administration was such that the memory of it still lives.

## CHAPTER III

### Song-hayan Empire and Askia the Great

Of all the black kingdoms of Soudan, Song-hay fur-
nishes the most interesting history.    A lack of space will
not allow us to give more than a brief narrative of this
most remarkable empire.

The people claim to be direct descendants of Sa, the
younger of the two sons of Mizraim, whom they claimed
first settled their empire.    According to the history of
the country, Sa devoted himself with the greatest interest
to his kingdom, which was given him by his father, and
made it prosperous.    He built towns for the mosques; he
constructed baths; he had palaces with stained glass windows and exquisite gardens; he erected statues bearing

burning glasses, and other marbles, along the Mediterranean coast.

Song-ha first attracts our attention in 1355, when
Ali-Kolon became king and delivered his people from
under the yoke of Melle. But Song-ha did not assert
her power as an influential kingdom until Sonni-Ali who
had been reared and educated at the court of Mansamusa, made his escape and returned to his native land
and freed his people from under the yoke of Melle.

The Song-ha people gladly welcomed Sonni-Ali as
their king. Under the rulership of this very energetic
king, Song-ha greatly extended her borders and became
the greatest country of Soudan.

Sonni-Ali was succeeded by his prime minister, Askia Mohammed, Abou Bekr. This man, says "Lady Lugard," was a pure blooded black Song-ha.

He was born of well known parents, in the island
Nina, a little below Sinder in the Niger, and he first made
his fame as a soldier, being one of the most distinguished
generals of Sonni-Ali's army. He was more remarkable
for qualities which usually characterize great civilians.
He apears to have been a man of liberal views, naturally
humane, and disposed to temperate justice with mercy,
more than usually cultivated, active, wise and firm. He
had been fortunate in the circumstances of his youth. He
came of good stock. His father was a man universally
respected. His mother was a woman of remarkable pi-
ety, who brought up her children with care. Thirty
years' experience, which he enjoyed as prime minister
to Sonni-Ali eminently fitted him for the high position of
king of the Song-ha empire. He assumed his authority
as king shortly after the death of Sonni-Ali, 1492, the

year that Columbus discovered America. Sonni-Ali had conquered the empire. The great work of Askia was to organize, to bring it into a condition of peace, prosperity and cultivation, which was little suspected as existing in the heart of Soudan, during a period which witnessed in Europe the expulsion of the Moors from Spain, the crusade of Charles V against the Saracens, the victory of Leepanto over the Turks and the closing of the principle ports of the Mediterranean to the infidels. One of his first acts was to organize a standing army. Simultaneously with his reform of the military forces of the empire he gave his attention to the church. The orthodox and pious, whose voices had not been heard during the late reign, came out of obscurity. Schools were founded, new mosques were built, and the new activity was felt throughout the empire. As soon as his subjects had become reconciled to the new conditions and peace and quiet had been established, Askia appointed his favorite brother to be regent in his place and went on a pilgrimage to Mecca and to seek at Cairo a formal investure at the hands of the Caliph of Egypt.

At this time Caliphs of Egypt still kept their position as the religious heads of the Mohammedan world. He received his investure at the hands of El Motarvekee XIV, Abassid Caliph of Egypt.

The ceremony consisted of a solemn abdication on Askia's part for three days of the Song-ha throne. On the fourth day the Caliph appointed him to the position of lieutenant Abasside of all the sultans in Soudan, and invested him in the sign of his authority, with a turban and cap. Askia remained for two years in the east, during which time he devoted much time to study. Among the subjects named as interesting his attention we find everything that concerned the government and the administra tion of the people.

Principles of taxation, and a special land tax, and the tithe are tributes to be taken from the newly conquered peoples; verification and inspection of weights and measures, regulation of trades, regulation laws of inheritance, laws for the suppression of fraud, custom and duties; laws for suppression of immorality and measures to be taken for the inheritance of better manners among the people. After remaining two years in the east, Asckai returned to his own empire. He succeeded in building up a very powerful empire of which Timbuctoo was capital.

This mysterious city reached its zenith during the reign of Asckai. Timbuctoo was a walled city of several thousand inhabitants. Within her walls stood large and stately mansions. Some one has said that there was a time when fortunes of gold could be gathered on her streets. The city was full of rich merchants. Her colleges and university produced some of the world's best scholars, lawyers, doctors and mechanics. The town, says Lady Lugard, swarmed with Soudanese students who were filled with ardor for knowledge and virtue. There were great stores of doctors, judges, priests and other men.

Mohammed Abou-Bekr tells of one of the noted black professors of Timbuctoo under whom it had been his good fortune to study. He speaks as follows: "He was one of the best of God's virtuous creatures. He was a working scholar and a man instinct with goodness. His nature was as pure as it was upright. Everyone

who knew him loved him. His whole life was given to
the teaching of others. He taught his pupils to love
science, to follow its teaching, to devote their time to it,
to associate with scholars and to keep their minds in a
state of docility. He occupied himself with what concerned him, listened to no gossip, and took no part in friv-
olity; but wrapped himself in a magnificent mantle of dis-
cretion and reserve. His hand held fast the standard of
continence."

The study of law, literature, grammar, theology and
science were the chief subjects taught in the schools of
Timbuctoo. There were also schools of medicine. It is
said that they believed in the maxim, "He who studies
anatomy pleases God." In 1618, the author of the Tar-
ikh mentioned the fact that a celebrated surgeon of Timbuctoo performed a successful operation on his brother
for cataract in 1816. There were noble philosophers
and astronomers in Timbuctoo.

Song-ha enjoyed her independence from 700 A. D. to
1591 A. D., a period of 891 years, during which she
wielded a powerful influence over the surrounding countries of the world. Ghana enjoyed an independent existence for over 1100 years.

Having briefly considered Timbuctoo and the Song-
ha empire, I now pass to the consideration of other kingdoms. The white man was surprised to find such evidences of civilization as existed among these native African tribes. Mr. Ogilby tells us the early African explorers reported the existence of several great kingdoms,
which have continued to exist down to the present time:
among which are Bornu, Bennin, Agades and Kano,
Ashanti, Sokoto, Fanti, Dahomi, Ibo and Bony. It may

be fitting right here to give a little description of the government of some of these black kingdoms.

Mr. Featherman has the following to say of the government of the kingdom of the Canuris of the millet zone: "The ruler of the Canuris was assisted in the administration by a chief counsellor or prime minister, a secretary of state, a commander in chief of the army, a minister of foreign affairs, who conducted the correspondence and regulated intercourse with strangers, a governor of the capital and the secretary of the interior who made annual tours throughout the empire, reporting upon the administration of the country, the condition of agriculture and industry.

In speaking of the government of the Hausa states Mr. Featherman says: "The executive officers of the Hausa states consisted of commander of cavalry, several judges, a chief of slaves, a minister of finance and a superintendent of beast of burden. The Hausa inflicted a death penalty for either murder or adultery. The Hausa had a law forbidding anyone from strolling about the streets at night, and an officer would arrest anyone committing such an offense. Any kind of rowdyism on the streets was strictly forbidden. Those found guilty were severely punished. In time of peace, robbery and murder were rare. Regular police preserved order at the markets. I might continue to give evidences of well organized systems of government in west Africa, which was found to be existing in a most flourishing condition before that part of the continent had ever been visited by a single representative of the Caucasian race—a civilization which was a production of negro brain, on his own virgin soil. A government existed among our African ancestors that equals the best system of government that may be found anywhere in our modern civilization.

---

## CHAPTER IV.

### The Black Dynasty of Spain

A very few people know, that for more than a half century, from 1086-1147, Spain was ruled by a black dynasty. After laying the foundation and establishing the town of Morocco, Yusuf Mache-fin crossed over into Spain. At this time the Arabs were being driven out of Spain. These men with tears in their eyes and sorrow in their hearts, came to Yusuf to employ his protection. Yusuf is described as being a wise and shrewd man. He could not speak the Arabic language, but spoke the African tongue. His army was made up of every tribe of the western desert. He drove the Christian forces out of southern Spain and established Yusuf's Spanish empire. Yusuf died in 1105. He was succeeded by his son as sultan of north Africa and Spain. This dynasty lasted, with a slight intermission, until 1147. A second African dynasty was established in 1150. Thus for a second time a purely African dynasty reigned upon the most civilized throne of Europe. He reconstructed the fleet of his predecessor and added to it not less than four hundred and sixty vessels. Monuments of the civil activities of these African rulers upon the Spanish soil still remain in the Tower of Gibraltar, which they built in 1160, and the great mosque of Seville which was begun in 1183.

### Abyssinia, the Modern Ethiopia

Let us leave western Africa and journey across the continent to the mountains of Abyssinia. One of the oldest kingdoms in the world is Abyssinia. It was one of the states of ancient Ethiopia. The queen of Sheba of Bible fame, who visited Solomon at a time when the Jewish empire was at its zenith, was queen of Shoa, in the southern part of Abyssinia. Abyssinia has never been wholly subjected to any foreign power. It is a rich and healthy country, inhabited by the descendants of the original Ethiopian stock. In speaking of Abyssinia, Sir Harry Johnson says: The very name which we apply to this modern Ethiopia is a Portuguese rendering of the Arabic, an ancient cant, for Habesh or negro. The French, Portuguese, Russians, Italians and English have all in their turn tried their fortunes in trying to bring this powerful Negro Kingdom under their subjection, but they all met with repeated reverses and have never been able to gain a permanent foot hold upon the soil of these aggressive black men, as the Abyssinians delight to call themselves. Italy was the last to give up the struggle. She proclaimed a protectorate over Abyssinia, which was recognized by England and Germany, but not by France and Russia. King John of Abyssinia, in 1882, sent Ras Allula with an army of 10,000 men against a smaller force of Italian troops and almost annihilated the entire army. The English government interceded in behalf of the Italian government and finally persuaded King John of Abyssinia to make peace with Italy. After this King John went to war aganst the Wahdist, another African nation, and was killed in battle. Menelik, the prince of Shoa, a vassal kingdom in the southern part of Abyssinia, proclaimed himself king. Menelik repudiated the protectorate of Italy over Abyssinia.

In the early spring of 1896 the Italian general Baratietri, with a large army, attempted to invade Abyssinia but he was met by the forces of Menelik in the vicinity of Adua, with the result that the Italian forces were defeated and cut to pieces with a terrible slaughter; many prisoners were taken. Sir Harry Johnson has the following to say about the effect of this battle on Europe: "This," says he, "was a terrible blow to Italy, and its effect upon European politics was far reaching." All thoughts of an Italian protectorate over Abyssinia were at an end, a position frankly acknowledged by Italy in her subsequent treaty of peace with Menelik. The French and Russians were very glad, and the French admiration of the black emperor, Menelik, exceeded all limits. A British ambassador was sent in 1887 to open up friendly relations with Abyssinia to establish a political agency at the king's court. The treaty at first sight seemed not wholly satisfactory to British interests, as it yielded a small portion of Samoa land to Abyssinia, and did not provide for any limitation to Abbyssinian boundaries on the west. Think of a proud nation like Great Britain entering to a treaty with a kingdom, and a black kingdom at that, when she conceded a larger concession than she received in return. The fact is that Great Britain has acknowledged that the black kingdom of Abyssinia has proven herself the peer of the most powerful European government. The prophecy of David, which says, "Princes shall come out of Egypt and Ethiopia shall soon stretch forth her hand unto God" is being fulfilled. The ancient Grecians regarded Ethiopia as being a people whose moral integrity secured for them the special favor and protection of Zeus.   When Zeus seemed to have forsaken the Grecian warriors in their effort to destroy the city of ancient Troy, Homer informs us through the Iliad, his famous poem, that Zeus was away on a visit to the country of the blameless Ethiopian.

## CHAPTER V.

### Some General Characteristics of the African Family

(1) His respect for leadership. It is a commendable fact that the different black families all over the African continent have their special leader.

Each tribe has its chief and each kingdom has its king.   These men are highly respected by their subjects. The reason why L'Overture was able to organize a band of black slaves to march against the well organized forces of the French government, defeat them in battle, and snatch the reigns of government from the hands of their former masters and establish the black republic of Hayti, because many of the black slaves, having been brought directly from Africa, had managed to keep themselves united under tribal chiefs, and by means of their secret societies to which they belong in their African homes; besides these there were hundreds of runaway slaves who kept themselves hid away in the dense forest of the island.

When the time came for action they all united under that matchless black general, Tour Saint L'Overture and defeated the French army.   The same black slaves many of whom were fresh from the jungles of Africa, established a black republic, which has continued to the present day.

### Race Pride.

The African black man has no desire to separate himself from his own people and country. He knows the traditional history of his ancestors and he verily believes that his is a superior race. The people of Abyssinia delight to call themselves black men. When some of the African natives had seen Mr. Stanley, he being the first white man that they had ever seen, they remarked that he was as white as the devil.

### Adaptability.

Perhaps the most pronounced general characteristics of the black man as a race are his adaptability to new conditions. Unlike the American Indian, who is becoming exterminated under the influence of modern civilization, the African black man is increasing in population and intelligence. In the colonies where European government has been established the natives enjoy the rights of citizenship and in many cases fill a large majority of the government positions. The standing armies are composed of native soldiers.

### The American Black Man in Slavery.

The history of the black man in America is so closely joined to the history of the country, it is difficult to separate one from another. We will first consider the black man as a slave. In 1619 a little Dutch vessel landed at Jamestown, Va., having for its cargo twenty black men who had been decoyed and brought here from the western coast of Africa. These black men were sold into slavery. This is the beginning of slavery in what is now the United States of America. It may be fitting to state here that all of the civilized nations of the world at some time during their history tolerated some form of slavery.

The black man himself in his African home has been the owner of slaves. Slavery still exists among some of the African tribes. I do not want it understood that I would for a moment endorse or sanction the institution of slavery, but I mention these facts to show that the people of the United States of America should not be considered the meanest people in the world because they once held our ancestors as slaves. Slave labor proved to be very profitable to the southern planters, and for this reason there rose a great demand for a large supply of slaves.

Slave labor was tried in the northern states, but proved unprofitable. The development of the southern section of the United States of America has been to a large extent the work of the black slaves. They felled the forest, planted, culivated and harvested the crops; in many cases manufactured the farming utensils, built wagons and carriages and houses for their masters. Their brawny arms have girded the continent with a belt of steel. In fact, they have played their part in every movement for the development of this country. When DeSoto made his cruel voyage through Florida, Georgia, Alabama, Mississippi, Arkansas and Louisiana, black men were with him. When Bal Boa discovered the Pacific ocean black men were there as witnesses to the event. It has already been shown in the preceeding chapters of this book that there have been some highly civilized black men upon the African continent from time immemorial. It may be interesting to the reader to know that some of the black men who were captured in Africa and brought to this country to be sold into slavery were men of rare intelligence. I have in mind a man who belonged to the Joloff nation, by the name of Job. His father was a king. Against the advice of his father, Job crossed into the territory of another nation ,which was hostile to the Joloffs. This prince was surprised and captured and the American slave vessel was near the place. The captain of the vessel bought Job with the hope of receiving a ransom from his father; but before the father had received the news and sent the ransom for his son, the prince, the vessel had sailed for America. Job was sold to a wealthy farmer near the city of Baltimore, Maryland. The farmer soon found out that Job knew absolutely nothing about farming, but discovered that he was an expert in caring for sheep and cattle. Job became dissatisfied with his condition and ran away. He was afterwards returned to his master. He could not speak the English language, but he found that some of his fellow slaves on the plantation understood his native language, to whom he related the story of his life. These slaves reported the matter to their master, whose sympathy and respectability caused him to surround Job with conditions which were more congenial. He provided him with a nice room and allowed him to enjoy more freedom. In the meantime, James Oglethorpe, who was then in London, England, heard of the misfortune of the prince, and sent over sufficient money to ransom him and pay bis passage to London, England. The master accepted the ransom and placed him on a vessel and sent him to London. He was received in London, not as a slave, but as a prince. He was Mohammedan and was very highly educated. He spoke the Arabic language fluently. He was highly entertained by the royal family. The founder of the British museum had some rare Arabic manuscripts that he got Job to translate. By this time Job had learned to speak the English language. It is said that Job reproduced two copies of the Koran, that he did not use the first in the reproduction of the second, but that he reproduced the whole from memory. The king fitted out a vessel and returned Job to his home. The subject of this sketch was captured in 1732, if I am not at fault regarding the date.

Many who will read this little book, are, no doubt, familiar with the story of the Amisted. The Amisted was a slave vessel which brought over some African slaves in 1839. Among those slaves there was a man by the name of Cinquez, under whose leadership the slaves overpowered the captain and crew and with weapons compelled the pilot to steer the vessel as they directed. They intended to return to Africa, but under cover of darkness the pilot pursued a northerly course. After several weeks Captain Green with one of the United States vessels captured the ship and took charge of Cinquez and his comrades. After a long legal proceeding, he and his companions were returned to Africa. John Quincy Adams pleaded two days of four and one half hours each before the supreme court to have the men released and returned to their home. Cinquez not only showed his great love for liberty but he also showed much bravery and executive ability. I simply cited these two cases to show what hundreds of others might have done under similar circumstances. There are several distinct characteristics which are peculiar to the African or black man. Among these are adaptibilty, durability and love of knowledge. Perhaps there is no other family in the

world that can so easily adapt itself to new things and
new conditions as the African or black family. It
seems to be an innate disposition on the part of the black
man to make the best of whatever condition in which he
finds himself. He not only conveniently adapts himself to
material things and conditions, but in addition to this it
had been proved that he lives happily side beside with
the people of any climate in the world. He is the only
people who can survive in the Soudan. Yet he lives with
equal ease and comfort in the temperate and frigid zones
as the nations that inhabit these regions. When Peary,
representing the Caucasian race of America, accomplished the matchless feat of crossing the icy plains of the
Arctic circle and planted the American flag upon the
north pole one Matthew Henson, an American black man,
was standing by his side. These are the only civilized
men who have stood upon the pivot upon which the world
is balanced. The Indian is being exterminated because
he cannot adapt himself to new conditions and assimilate
the civilization of the American white man. The black
man has not only been able to live and multiply along by
the side of the white man, but he also assimilated the
civilization of the white man, even in the days of slavery.
A love for liberty caused many of the slaves to work and
purchase their liberty and the freedom of their families.
Many of these free black men worked and acquired considerable property. I shall mention a few of the free
black men who distinguished themselves in North Carolina, whose histories are related by Prof. John Spencer
Bassett, Ph. D., in his book entitled "Slavery," in the
state of North Carolina. John C. Stanley was a black
slave belonging to Mistress Lydia Stewart. John was a

barber by trade and was such a faithful servant that his mistress gave him his freedom in 1808.  He soon began to acquire black slaves and land until he had sixty-four slaves and many more bound free black persons on his several plantations.  He was very apt in business, and made money by shaving notes for his white neighbors. His fortune is said to have amounted to forty thousand dollars.  His home was Newburn, North Carolina.  It is said that he never forgot the kindness of his mistress in setting him free, but that when she became old he took great pleasure in conducting her through the streets of Newburn.  She attended the Presbyterian church every Sunday morning, leaning upon the arm of her former servant.

The sense of gratitude shown by this man is characteristic of the black people.  There were several other thrifty slave holding black men in and around Newburn, among whom were: John Good, a barber; John Green, a carpenter and contractor; Richard Hazel, a blacksmith; Scipio Hughes, a blacksmith and owner of a livery stable; Fellow Bragg, a successful tailor.  What was true of the black men in Newburn, N. C., was true of the black men in many other states.  The free black men of the United States of America owned $2,500,000 worth of property when Lincoln issued the Emancipation Proclamation.  We might mention Washington Spradley of Louisville, Kentucky, who was worth at his death $350,000, a barber by trade, and Fannie Kennedy, a black woman who was very wealthy and had property all over Louisville.  What was true of the above mentioned was true of many others in all the states.  Space will not allow me to name them individually though we know many of them personally.

A desire or love for knowledge is an innate quality of the black man. Even in the days of slavery, when it was a crime for any one to teach the black man to read or write, we find many of them, by some means, acquiring at least the rudiments of an education. I wish to speak particularly of one character found in Prof. Johnson's school history, who is a black man, and also Prof. Bassett's book named above. The name of this man is Rev. John Chavous. He was born of free parents in Granville county, near Oxford, North Carolina, about 1763. He was a full blooded black man. When he was but a boy, he attracted the attention of the white members and officials of the Presbyterian church, who decided to send him to Princeton college, just to see if a black man really possessed the ability to acquire a classical education. He completed the course with honor and finally returned to his native state and opened a classical school in Granville exclusively for the children of wealthy white farmers of the community.

We all know that Princeton is in New Jersey over which college Ex-President Wilson was president. He also taught in Wake and Chatham counties. Among his pupils were William P. Mangum, afterward U. S. senator and Priestly H. Mangum, his brother; Archibold and John Henderson, sons of Chief Justice Henderson; Charles Manly, afterward governor of the state; Dr. James L. Woretham of Oxford, N. C., and many more excellent men. He was honored and respected by all who knew him. Such was the accomplishment of a black man, born just 100 years before Lincoln issued the

Proclamation of Emancipation. What Mr. Chavous accomplished might have been done by hundreds of others had they been given an equal opportunity.

---

## CHAPTER VI.

### The Religious Life of the Slaves

All of the slaves who were brought from Africa to this country were either pagans or Mohammedans. Generations of contact with Christian civilization had the remarkable effect of stamping out many of the fetish and idolatrous notions of the African. In a large measure, the slave accepted the God and Savior of their masters. Many of them were very sincere in their devotions. They possessed that simple Christ-like faith. Many of the burdened hearts of the slaves were made light because they knew how to cast their cares upon Jesus. The race produced some strong preachers in the days of slavery. The old historic town of Fayettesville, N. C. bears the distinction of having Methodism first introduced into it by Henry Evans, a black preacher. In speaking of Rev. Evans, Bishop Caphers said: I have known not many preachers who appeared more conversant with the scriptures than Henry Evans, all of whose conversation was more instructive as to the things of God. Ralph Freeman was another black man who won distinction as a preacher in the days of slavery. He was a native of Anson county, N. C., and was often called on to preach funerals and preach at Associations. He was a Baptist preacher. I have already referred to John Chavous, who was a Presbyterian minister, educated at Princeton, N. J.

We will not omit to mention among the distinguished

ante bellum preachers, Richard Allen, the founder of
the A. M. E. church. Rev. Allen was born in 1760 He
bought his freedom. On April 17, 1787, the colored people of Philadelphia, under the leadership of Allen and
Jones, formed what was known as the Free African Sj-
ciety. Out of this society grew the A. M. E. church,
which was organized by Rev. Allen in 1816. They first
worshipped in a blacksmith shop. Such was the beginning of one of the greatest religious organizations that
we have in this country. The history of Bishop Allen is
too well known to repeat it. I would not close this sketch
on the religious life of the black man in slavery without
saying a word at least about Sojourner Truth. This
unique character was born in 1775; was brought when a
child from Africa and sold as a slave in the state of New
York. Her mother became a very devoted Christian.
She taught her children to love and fear the Lord. Sojourner Truth secured her freedom and became a great
advocate for the rights of women. Wendell Philipps
said that he knew but one human being who could bring
down a whole audience by a few simple words, and that
was Sojourner Truth. She never failed to seize an opportunity to use all of her power of persuasion for the abolition of slavery in the United States of America.

## CHAPTER VII.

### The Black Man After the Emancipation

When Abraham Lincoln signed the Proclamation, September 22, 1862, that brought freedom to 4,000,000 of black men, he little knew of the wonderful possibilities of the people whom he had freed.

The emancipated black man was without experience of self reliance and self government. He found himself confronted with new conditions, but he gradually began to adapt himself to his new surroundings. Freedom without the right of citizenship is only part freedom. Congress hastened to pass the 13th, 14th and 15th amendments to the Constitution, making the black man a citizen and at the same time giving him the right of suffrage. There were many who condemn the government for indiscriminately granting the right of suffrage to the newly emancipated slaves. While this was a very advanced step, it was the best thing that could have been done under the circumstances. The ballot in the hands of the masses of people is their only defense against the curtailing or encroachment upon their rights as citizens. We admit that the management in some of the states was far from being ideal but this state of affairs cannot be truthfully laid at the door of suffrage. Some of the carpet baggers, were, no doubt, corrupt in their practices in the administration of the government of some of the southern states. It must also be admitted that they used the ignorant freed men as a tool to aid them in carrying out their evil practices. But there was no other means by which the liberty of the emancipated slaves might have been safe guarded except by placing into their hands the ballot, the only weapon by which the rights and the liberties of a people may be protected.

At the close of the war many of the black men who had gone into the northern states and secured an education returned to the southern states and became political leaders among their people. Among those who distinguished themselves were Ex-Congressman John M. Langston, P. B. S. Pinchback, who became acting governor of Louisiana, Josiah T. Settle, Frederick Douglas, of abolition fame, Ex-Senator B. K. Bruce, and a host of others, which lack of space prevents me from mentioning. All of these gentlemen not only reflected credit upon themselves and the people to whom they belonged, but they also reflected honor upon the nation at large. A revolution has taken place in the politics of the south. A wholesale effort has been made to eliminate the black man from politics. No well informed black man will object to the enactment of such laws as may be necessary to improve the citizenship of the country, and to place the ballot into the hands of such as are interested in good government, provided these laws have equal force over all classes of citizens regardless of people or previous condiiton of servitude.

I do not agree with that class of men who believe that the black man should be eliminated from politics. I believe that taxation is just as intolerable and unjust today as it was in the days of Patrick Henry and Thomas Jefferson. No people should be denied the right of representation in a government which they are taxed to support. The black man constitutes nearly two tenths of the population of the United States without a single representative in the nation's Congress. Such conditions should not exist in a republican form of government, which is supposed to be a government of the people, for the people and by the people.

### His Material Advancement

In Georgia alone the black man owns 1,449,624 acres of land, valued at $7,972,787. It is estimated that the black men of the United States own at least 30,000 square miles of farm land. Deal Jackson of Albany, Ga., owns and works 2,000 acres of land, upon which he employs forty-six families. For the last ten or twelve years Mr. Jackson has been the first man to place a bale of cotton upon the market. Alfred Smith, of Oklahoma, better known as the cotton king, won the first prize at the World's Exposition at Paris, 1900. John J. Benson, of Alabama, owns a farm of 3,000 acres. J. G. Grove, the black potato king, raises an average of 72,150 bushels of potatoes each year, which is an average of 245 bushels to the acre. He owns five farms. The black men of the United States of America own and control about seventy banks. A report from twenty-nine of these banks shows a deposit of $1,051,770, and a surplus of about $200,000. It is estimated upon reliable information that the black man of the United States of America owns taxable property, valued at $550,000,000. Adding to this amount $300,500, which he has deposited in the banks of this country, to say nothing of the amount hid away in chimney corners and under mattresses, will make a grand total of 900,000,000 of wealth owned by the black man of the United States of America.

### The Black Mechanics

In 1900 there were over 200,000 black men engaged in work requiring skill. Among them were miners and quarry men, 36,568; saw mill and planing mill employees, 33,266; dress-makers, 24,110; carpenters, 21,-114; barbers and hairdressers, 19,948; tobacco and cigar operators, 15,349; brick and stone masons, 14,387; iron and steel workers, 2,327; engineers and firemen, 10,227; blacksmiths, 10,004; brick and tile makers, 9,970. In addition to these there were 2,585 black operatives in factories and mills, 52 architects and designers, 185 electricians; 120 engineers and surveyors; 1,262 machinists, 198 tool and cutlery makers, 342 cabinet makers, 109 clock and watchmakers, 66 gold and silver workers, 86 book binders, 22 engravers, 1,845 tailors, 15 glove makers, 24 model and pattern makers, 247 photographers, and 1,045 upholsterers.

### The Black Professional Men.

There are about 30,000 black teachers of schools and colleges. Of this number of efficient and consecrated teachers, Dr. Booker T. Washington and Dr. W. E. B. Dubois rank among the foremost educators of the world  There are about 70,000 black ministers, 2,000 physicians, 1,000 lawyers, 100 literary and scientific persons and 210 journalists. We have had some very able representatives of all the professional men and women of our people. Among them are to be found Dr. R. F. Boyd, of Nashville, Tennessee, Dr. Daniel H. Williams, of Chicago, one of the two known surgeons of the world who have performed successful operations upon the human heart, Dr. George H. Hall, of Chicago, and Dr. A. M. Curtis of Washington, D. C., noted surgeons of our people, Dr. Garland Penn, secretary of the Epworth League of the M. E. church, among the colored people of the United States of America. Space will not allow me to make full mention of Paul Lawrence Dunbar, who is reckoned among the greatest poets of the world, Henry O. Tanner, the black artist whose productions, "The Raising of Lazarus," "The Ten Virgins" and "The Lord's Supper," have won the applause and admiration of the world's best critics. Mr. Tanner won the gold medal at the World's Exhibition at Paris, France. Rev. Dr. E. C. Morris, president of the African National Baptist Convention, which is the largest organization of our people in the world, Rev. Dr. R. H. Boyd, secretary of the National Baptist Publishing Board, which is located at Nashville, Tennessee, and is valued at $200,050, the Rev. Dr. C. E. Walker, the Baptist minister, the black Spurgeon, Bishop Turner of the A. M. E. church, and Bishop Waters of the A. M. E. Zion church, Dr. Mason of the M. E. church and a host of others whom a lack of space prohibits my naming.

The civilization of a people may be measured by the contribution they make toward the establishment of schools and churches. The black people of the United States of America own property valued at $50,000,000 and school property at $20,000,000. Since 1880 black churches have contributed $15,000,000 for the education of our people. In addition to this, Mr. Carnegie stated in his address at Edinburg, Scotland, in 1907, that the cost of running the public schools in 1907 was $1,345,859, and that the black people contributed by means of taxation, $1,496,036 which was $150,137 more than was expended in the common schools for the black people of that year. Thus we see that the black man not only paid for his own education but he also contributed more than $150,000 for the education of the white boys and girls of these United States of America. It has been clearly shown that the black people are not backward, neither do they show any signs of becoming extinct. But he is justly recorded among the advanced people of the world. A people that can produce such men as Toursaint L'Overture, St. Augustine the bishop of Hippo Africa, Ira Aldrige, whose success as an actor, caused the king of Prussia, 1854, to confer a declaration upon him; Dumas, the half breed black man of the West Indies, who became one of the most famous novelists of France, the national poet of Russia, Alexander Sergeilvich Pushkin, although of noble birth, his mother was a mixed blooded African; Pixley Isaka Seme, the Zulu who came directly from Africa and completed the college course of Columbia University of New York and carried off the oratorical honors of his class in competition with America's brightest sons, in 1907, justly deserves to take rank among the highly civilized people of the earth.

If after reading this little book some black boy is made to have a better opinion of himself and of the people with whom he is identified, the writer will feel that he has accomplished the purpose which he had in view.

REV. JOSEPH JULIUS JACKSON, D. D.,

Bellefontaine, Ohio.

Dedicated to the memory of his sainted mother and father, namely: Henry and Emmaline Jackson and to his two sainted wives Hattie E. and Bertha B. Jackson, the late Rev. S. W. Lott, my teacher and preceptor, and all friends who have contributed to my advancement and elevation. God bless their memories.

www.ingramcontent.com/pod-product-compliance
Lightning Source LLC
Chambersburg PA
CBHW071759020426
42331CB00008B/2325